Into Me I See.

9 PERSPECTIVES THAT WILL SHIFT YOUR REALITY INTO THE ONE THAT YOU'VE ALWAYS DREAMT

By

ELEXIS MEEKS

Elexis Meeks. Into Me I See © All Rights Reserved. Mind Over Matter Universal Press 10.10.2020

Table of Contents

Acknowledgments		3
Introduction	Into Me I See	5
Chapter 1	Embracing All That I Am	9
Call to Action	Believing	24
Chapter 2	The Power of Agreement	26
Call to Action	Activating Your Power of Agreement	34
Chapter 3	Victim to Witness Concept	35
Call to Action	Shifting from Victim to Witness	58
Chapter 4	It Takes a Community	59
Call to Action	Knowing Your Community	64
Chapter 5	Everything Happens for a Reason	66
Call to Action	Finding A Solution	71
Chapter 6	Speak Life into Existence	72
Call to Action	Speaking Life into Existence	81
Chapter 7	Eye Create Abundance	88
Call to Action	Manifesting Your Desires	98
Chapter 8	Conscious Choices	99
Call to Action	Getting Clear on What You Want	104
Chapter 9	Be in Your Power	105
Call to Action	Being in Your Power	110
About the Author	Meet "Ajai Alai"	111

Acknowledgments

All praises to the Most High for all He has done. I am extremely grateful to be a representative of God's promise. I am grateful He saw fit for me to be a safe container to hold this much needed conversation. He provided me with the resources I need to have this book materialize regardless of the crisis of the pandemic we are currently in. That alone is enough to be grateful for. This book is dedicated to my children A'Lyria, Tyvon Jr., and DeMari. Thank You for being God's example of unconditional love, faith, and forgiveness. It is with much gratitude that I get to experience heaven on earth because of you. Thank You.

To my twin sisters Tereya and Terriah. The both of you are the living water that continues to flow through my body, thank you for simply being you! To my Mom and Dad, I am greatly appreciative for bringing me here to earth.

To the leading men in my life: my Father, Terry Adderley, my cousin who has always been a father figure, Larry Balfour, and my bonus dad, Morris Redd. I am grateful for your unconditional love and support. It has physically kept me grounded on earth's surfaces during troubling times.

To my mentors who were passionately committed to my transformation. Lisa Nichols and Lakeisha Michelle, I Thank You with all my heart for caring enough about me to be honest with me and share your world of wisdom so that I can undoubtedly grow into the next best version of myself. You both are a breath of fresh air and a shining light in the midst of my darkness. Thank You.

Much appreciation to my editor Morris Redd for the countless, tireless hours of doing what editors do. I am often grateful for his patience and persistence. Without his valuable input, this book would not be the helpful guide that it is. I am grateful to have a powerful, conscious giver at hand. Additionally, I am appreciative of my Earth Angels of viewers for their meaningful feedback.

And of course, YOU! I am ever grateful for your open mind and your hunger for getting to that next best version of that unique and amazing creation called YOU!

Introduction

The Lotus flower is regarded in many different cultures, especially in eastern religions, as a symbol of purity, enlightenment, self-regeneration and rebirth. Its characteristics are a perfect analogy for the human condition: even when its roots are in the dirtiest waters, the Lotus produces the most beautiful flower. ***The reason I have selected lotus flower at the top of each page is to remind you that you can blossom into the beautiful flower that you are regardless of your circumstances.***

Into Me I See

Be crazy enough to believe that you deserve it all. Lisa Nichols

Peace, Love, and Light to you.

Are you ready to embark upon a journey of everlasting happiness and abundance? Have you always known yourself to be more than your current situation? Are you ready to dive deep and become all that you were born to be? If you've answered yes to any of these questions, you are in the right place at the right time!

INTO ME I SEE was written with one ultimate purpose: to *help you help yourself* on the journey to becoming your next best version. It is my prayer that when you are faced with a difficult or traumatic challenge, you will implement the *9 Perspectives* that are detailed throughout this book. With continuous and spirited application of these perspectives, you will shift your reality into one that you love.

While preparing for this extraordinary journey to everlasting peace, love, happiness, and abundance, you are going to have to leave your old baggage behind. When I say baggage, I am speaking of those old beliefs that no longer serve you. Oh, and you won't be needing that beautiful sparkling mask of perfection, either. You are about to become a new person, with a fresh set of garments, and a confident-glowing countenance. If it is your desire and intent to do so, you are about to be transformed in all manner of your life, simply through the renewing of your mind.

I like to believe we all grow through challenging times in our lives. I am excited to tell you that you are not alone, AND that you already have divine power within you to transform your life. I have embodied and continue to apply the *9 Perspectives* in which I will be sharing with you, in this book, to shift my own reality into one that I love. The **9 Perspectives That Will Shift Your Reality Into The One That You've Always Dreamt** are: (1) Embracing All That I Am, (2) The Power of Agreement, (3) Victim to Witness Concept, (4) It Takes a Community, (5) Everything Happens for a Reason, (6) Speak Life into Existence, (7) Eye Create Abundance, (8) Conscious Choices, and (9) Be in Your Power.

As for me and my house, I choose to serve God. I came to the inner-standing that there is a higher energy/frequency in which we all have access to. This all-knowing, higher energy is also commonly referred to by God, Higher Self, YOUniverse, or Source. You may use whatever label you wish, but the truth of the matter is that this higher power dwells inside of us all. When you think about it, everything is made up of energy. Energy cannot be created or destroyed, but it can change form. Remember that when you start to apply the principles in this book.

You will be figuratively and literally changing the composition of your energy. Everything possesses energy, even a rock. All we must do is tap into it in the right way and align ourselves to the frequency that supports our desires. Effectively put into progressive use, tapping into our full energy source can have us creating and realizing all that we wish to be, do, and have. Personally, I do not buy into religion, per se, for I believe it was introduced to keep us separated as a people. My religion is love. In my Bible, "Love rejoices with truth (1 Cor 13:6) and "We are to do everything in love (1 Cor 16:14). Anyway, by giving you a look into my experience, my main objective is to share my love by helping you tap into the everlasting abundance in your YOUniverse, as I was able to do. Now that you've decided to invite everlasting abundance into your YOUniverse, it is time to put in some work! Please make sure you keep a pen and paper nearby, as you read this book. Remember, there are many Calls to Action within. If you are to experience change, you must be the change. Let's put it this way, if you want something, you have to do something. Got your pen? Welcome to ***Into Me I See***.

Embracing All That I Am

Recognize the Treasure that Make You You

      I remember my freshman year at Boynton High, although I only knew about 3 people which included my sister and my cousin. I can honestly say my high school experience was a reflection of the magical high school experience you usually see on television. The beautiful, thick, popular, varsity cheerleader, whose boyfriend was a star football player: That was me. I was a leader in the student council. I participated in basketball, flag football, and weightlifting to keep my body in shape during the off-season. While dancing in the band, I was selected to be a freshmen leader. Regardless of how many times I skipped class, the administrators always had my back, including the Principal. Everything just worked in my favor, like that. I was just that cool.

"I am a Tiger, I am proud to be a Tiger; We are a family that depends on each other. I respect my coach, my teammates, myself, and my school; This team is as solid as I am and I will do everything I possibly can to keep it that way, remaining dedicated, positive, and a team with no excuses. Proud TIGER!"

That was the chant we embodied before departing on or off the field. The rush I got from yelling and rooting for our players was one thing. But being at the front of those stands showing off my skills had the best of me! For the first time, I felt like I truly belonged. I grew up in a house where my mother and Dad lived. Wait! Before we continue let me make this clear. I have two Dads. My biological Dad goes by the name Snoop. During most of my childhood, my biological father was in and out of prison, finding his own way. My stepdad goes by the name Terry. He has been there for me since the age of 2. Whether he was with my Mom or not, he never left my side. That is who I will be referring to as my Dad, when referring to my biological Dad you'll hear me say Snoop. Now, where were we? Growing up with my Mom, Dad, and sisters was pretty fun and adventurous. Although Mom and Dad practically lived from paycheck to paycheck, they made sure me, and my 5 sisters had what we needed and sometimes got what we wanted. Orlando FL was like our second home. We visited just about every theme park in town, including our favorite theme park of all, Fun Spot. It clearly makes sense why that would be our favorite place to visit. My parents loved it too. It was cheap and tons of fun for everyone! Dad was the main disciplinarian. As soon as things got out of order, whether we were fighting over a game, or not listening, Daddy would tell us to find a corner and stand in it. While Mom did her best to save us from the corner horror, Daddy usually prevailed. LOL!

Mom had a different way of loving me and my sisters. I was sure that if you looked up my Mom's in the dictionary, you would find her picture posted with the words loving, sweet, and cool as its definition - at least, that was the experience that others would recount. However, that was not necessarily my experience. She seemed to have a special love and kindness toward everyone. My Mom would easily win the *Citizen of the Year Award* every year, had it been up to society. I often felt like I didn't necessarily "belong" in the family. I would always ask God why me? Me and my older sister, Esther, would fist fight over EVERYTHING, whether it was a bag of chips or a fork. I'd like to say, Mom always took Esther's side. I'm not sure if it was because she was her first child or what. However, the story I told myself was, Mom was not too fond of me because I had a thing for girls, which Mom did not agree with at all! Whatsoever, I felt like I could not be myself with Mom, so I often ran away from home to have the freedom to be, though that only lasted a few days. My short-lived freedom ended once they sent out text messages to all my friends, in search for me, ultimately finding me and making me come back home. My Dad and I shared an extraordinarily strong, transparent relationship. Although he did not always agree with me, he allowed me to have my own opinion and afforded me the opportunity to bump my head a few times. He always supported me along the way.

After growing through certain stages in life, in search for myself, it allowed me to come to the realization that my Mom, Dad and everyone else, for that matter, honestly does the best that they can with what they know. And hey, if that is so, then why on earth would I want to fault them for simply doing what they know how? We must learn to see people the way that God sees us, and that is in the eyes of love. Love says I accept you for you, flaws and all. Love says I respect the divine God that guides you. And, I choose to accept you just as you are no matter what your B.S (belief system).

My freshman year at Boynton High, I remember stepping on campus seeing signs everywhere that read the time had come to audition for homecoming court.

The directions stated that candidates had to present their talent before a group of judges and an audience. We also had to model in the homecoming fashion show, which was organized by the student council. Gasp! That had *Elexis* written all over it, I thought. With my mouth open wide, "sign-me up!" I blurted.

Weeks flew by after preparing my performance, handing my make-shift flyers out of index cards with candy attached, saying **Vote for Meeks!** The day had come. It was audition day! I was so excited! Blood rushed through my veins. "Up next is Elexisss Meeeeeeeeeks" the host blurted. I felt my heart drop to my stomach.

After, dancing and cheering my heart out, one of the contestants whispered "May the baddest chick win." Completely stunned, "whatever that means," I mumbled. Gazing into the room, I could feel my knees getting ready to cave in as the host began, "The votes are in. May I get a drum roll please? And the Duchess of 2009-2010 Winner is Elexis Meeks!!" Screaming in total shock, Y E S S! I did it! As they queened me with the winning crown, I cheered, with a kool-aid smile lighting up the room. Now, to brag to my fat friends. LOL! Fat friends, you may ask...? Who would call their friends "fat"? Lex.Bo, We.Bo, and Ty.Bo, that's who! The fattest friends you've seen and I'm not talking weight. Our little Bo crew had three classes together, Mr. McElwain, Ms. Glenn, and Mr. Coach Floyd.

> **No one wants to do something solely because they "have to." When we tell ourselves, we "get to" do something, we draw in a happy, excited energy of expectation.**

I know you may ask, why would I put two prefixes before someone's name. Well, it is because Mr. Coach Floyd was my science teacher and the varsity football coach. And I have a habit of renaming people, so he became Mr. Coach Floyd. Before entering either of the classes we shared, we knew if one of us came with no snacks, it was trouble in paradise. This meant that the person who showed up with no snacks got to provide snacks for two days in a row. Notice how I said, "got to" instead of "had to." When we tell ourselves that we have to do something, that brings a negative energy with it, because it adds obligation to the situation instead of willingness. No one wants to do something solely because they "have to." When we tell ourselves, we get to do something, we draw in a happy, excited energy of expectation. Take a moment to try this on for yourself. Write about something you feel you have to do that you are not so happy about. Write the cons that will happen if you don't do it. Then, show gratitude and have an attitude like you get to do that thing instead of that you have to do it. What did you think? *Throughout this book, you will find various Calls to Action. Please make sure that you use this book as a tool, a resource, and a guide, and you do each of the Calls.*

Buss down, Buss down. That was our crew's theme song that we created in reference to food. We treated each other like family, in fact we were more like Bonnie and Clyde. We.Bo and I did everything we could to keep Ty.Bo out of trouble, but trouble always seemed to find him, at least that's what I thought. Not only did we share snacks, we shared secrets, homework, you name it. Nobody could mess with the Bos, in fact everyone wanted to join in on our super cool crew. Toward the end of freshman year, I was devastated when I found out that my best friend, Ty.Bo, was moving to Nebraska because the courts felt it would be best for him to focus on school and work on his behavior. Ty.Bo was being sent to this place called Boystown. I remember sitting in Ms. Glenn's class when they called for Tyron's dismissal. I said my last goodbye waving at him from outside the classroom. Entering Mr. Coach Floyd's class after Ty's dismissal, I sat next to Pooh Bear who was a great friend of mine, more like a brother, so we could chat. With excitement, I said 'Bro, you know what would be crazy? If Tyron walked in right now saying, "sike, I ain't goin' nowhere." That was just the type of person Tyron was, always making jokes and trying to fool somebody. Approximately 3 minutes later, Tyron enters the room, "I'm baaaaaaaaack!" he yelled. You will soon learn that there are no coincidences. Bursting into tears, "I thought you were leaving," I sobbed. "Nah, you know I had to come back and say goodbye one last time," he said. Although Tyron moved to Nebraska, we kept in contact sending letters back and forth with one day per week to talk on the phone. As time went by, we began catching feelings for each other and before you knew it, we were in a relationship. Yes! ... me and my best friend were now one. Toward the end of junior year, a longtime friend of mine named Casandra asked me to join The Purple Diamond Dancers which were a part of the auxiliary in the band. Yo! that would be lit, but I knew Coach Millie and Tyron would kill me. They'll never let me get away with this one. Although we all represented the same school, it was like war between the band and the cheerleaders. At the football games, we felt as if the band was trying to outshine us instead of complementing us. It seemed like every time we called set to begin our cheer, the band started cranking up. I knew if I joined the band, I'd be stepping on toes. After Mr. Coach Milsap's class, Tyron and I met at our regular spot, where the Bo's linked up after every class, directly in front of building 7, to talk about my decision to join the dancers. Now, it was time for the infamous question that I practically already knew the answer to. I spotted Tyron cheesing and waiting for my arrival. I told him I was glad to see him in good spirits. "How would you feel if I joined the dance team?" Looking stunned, he appeared to be waiting for me to say April fools in the

Elexis: The Band Dancer, Cheerleader, and the 2014 Homecoming Queen

middle of May. "Yeah, you got me messed up. If you join the team, we are no longer together." Feeling sad, "okay, never mind," I mumbled.

Later that summer, revelation popped in my head. "Elexis, you are a dancer. You have one chance to be a senior in High School. You better make the absolute best of it." Or, as RuPaul would say, "You Better WORK!" The very next day I asked Cassandra where to sign-up? Realizing I only had one day to get prepared, I went to work. Feeling anxious, and very paranoid, negative thoughts flooded my mind. "Will I even make the cut? I haven't danced in over 3 years. Do I still have what it takes?

It was audition day! After learning the choreography in approximately two hours, the votes were in. Your girl made the team! Not only did I make the team, I scored the highest points with Mr. Velez, the Band Director, Mrs. Berry, the Dance Coordinator, and two alums as judges. Although I have always known myself to be a dancer, I felt much gratitude about making the team, as the days went by after the auditions. Now, being part of the auxiliary of the band, Mrs. Berry, our coach, invited the team to a Zumba class at her local gym, the YMCA. After taking a short break from dancing, the Zumba instructor directed us to get ready and take our places again. As I stood in position, ready to dance, an older lady came to me and very aggressively said, "move! you're in my spot." Immediately, I offered my apologies and stood in an empty space nearby, continuing to dance. Later when we arrived back at the school to continue our practice, Ms. Berry stated "I'd like to announce our freshmen leader, Elexis Meeks. I want to congratulate you on how you handled the situation earlier today." I did not even know that she was paying attention. Overly

2014 Purple Diamond Dancers. Freshmen Leader and The Tail

filled with joy I burst into tears. So, there I was, the freshmen leader of the band. Not only was I the freshman leader, but I was also awarded best dancer that year.

Although my parents didn't have the resources to support my activities, I was very fortunate to be blessed with teachers, coaches and even the principal, who supported me financially along the way. I was having the time of my life. To add the icing to the cake, during my senior year, I ran for Homecoming Queen. While I was confident that I would come out on top, I knew that my competition was this girl named Nyla, whose mother was a guidance counselor at Boynton High. Although

Nyla was fairly new to Boynton High, her mother had the authority to call a revote, and she exercised it. I never would have imagined that she had an upper hand, at least not in terms of a competitive edge, but I quickly learned about the politics of school pageants. Nevertheless, once the votes were in and your girl came out on top, that all changed very quickly. Thankfully, I was crowned 2014 Homecoming Queen of Boynton High School.

On graduation day, our dream had come true, I was pregnant! "Finally," we thought, "now we would have the opportunity to build as a family. Both Tyron and I had come from dysfunctional families and now we were afforded the chance to do things differently than what we had come from. In addition, personally, I would have a little person that would love me unconditionally and never leave my side. My beautiful princess, Lyri, was born in December and then my second blessing, my handsome little prince, Duke, came a year and a half later. A few months after Duke's birth, along with Tyron, their dad, we moved to Daytona FL to start a new life. My hope was that our move would create a life that we would love and be proud of. Unfortunately, yet very divine, things did not turn out as planned. I quickly found myself in an abusive, toxic, and self-destructive relationship. There were days when I would look in the mirror and cry my eyes out. I didn't recognize the woman that was reflecting in that mirror. I saw someone who looked more like a crackhead. I used marijuana as a way of escape

Freshmen year as The Homecoming Duchess

from reality. Funny thing is, as soon as the high went away, I was back in my reality. I was disgusted with myself. How did I go from this beautiful, athletic, and smart leader to a scorned woman that was vulnerable, depressed, and feeling ugly?

After 6 months of living in Daytona, I came to a clear inner-standing that I had a strong support system at home and home was where I needed to be. There was no purpose in caring for my entire household by myself. It was exhausting and depressing. I finally gained the strength to walk away from Tyron and from the situation that I was in. One day after coming home from work, I announced, "I'm moving back to West Palm Beach." And I did just that. It's funny because I remember always putting the blame on the "devil". I always felt like the devil was attacking me, or out to get me. It wasn't until I decided to take ownership, and responsibility for the life I had created for myself. Only then was I able to let in other perspectives, choosing what resonated within me. Carlton Spann said it best in his book of poetry *Inspired By God*, "Sometimes, I might not do the things, say the right words, but I try to be careful of what I'm doing. Yes, I may be hurt. Guess what, remember, I'm only human." Now, what will you choose?

CALL TO ACTION: Believing

Write a short phrase of something that you want to achieve, whether it is something like getting a bicycle, a cup of coffee, or even a pay increase. Add details such as a date that the goal will be achieved. Make sure it is something attainable.

Ex: I will have $200 within three days.

Because you may have absolutely no idea where this money is going to come from, things will come up against the idea of you having what you said will happen. While inhaling cultivating affirmations and exhaling the ensuing malnourishing thoughts, take notice of adversarial imaginings, people, and situations.

So shall my word be that goes out from my mouth; it shall not return to me empty, but it shall accomplish that which I purpose, and shall succeed in the thing for which I sent it (**Isaiah 55:11**).

I have done this exercise numerous times. You can go as far as detailing your strategy if you have an intended strategy, but that is not a prerequisite for this to necessarily manifest.

For example: You may say, "On July 31st, I will have in my possession $200 in cash, which will come by way of my doing hair.

Try this with several things. Start with small desires. Remember, it was through practice, however unintentional it may have been, that you perfected getting what you did not want. You kept speaking things and believed those things, and they came true. You kept saying to yourself that you were broke and believed that you were not going to have enough money as was the usual case. And, guess what? You remained broke and "enough" money never materialized, as you had repeatedly declared.

The Power of Agreement

Living in Your Authenticity

For a moment, think about the meaning of *Agreement*: harmony or accordance in opinion or feeling; a position or result of agreeing. Now pause, no, really... pause... take a moment to really grasp and inner-stand or as I like to say, inner-stand the meaning of agreement. In every situation there is always an underlying conversation that we have with ourselves. Eighty percent of the time, that conversation comes from our subconscious mind where we aren't fully aware, yet it dictates our feelings and actions. When I think about the meaning of agreement, it reminds me that our entire "belief system" is based upon agreement. A belief system is a set of principles or tenets which together form a basis of religion, philosophy, or moral code. Think about it, before we are even able to form our first words, the people who care for us have already begun to shape our belief systems based on theirs. They intentionally and unintentionally impose their beliefs on us, based on what they know and or to what they've agreed to. Basically, they model how to be like them. We are domesticated the way animals are through a system of rewards and punishments, commendation, and condemnation. We are told that we are a "good girl" or a "good boy" when we do what our trainers want us to do and we're a "bad girl" or "bad boy" when we don't do what they want us to do. Our belief system is based on how we perceive our past experiences. You and I both know that everyone experiences life differently, yet we still seem to assert our individual beliefs as if it is the only way of thinking or better yet, the "right way" of thinking. You will soon see how everything you believe or agree with is merely your way of viewing things, and it does not necessarily mean that it is right or wrong. It is all simply B.S! – a Belief System. The wonderful thing about all of this is that we possess the Power of Agreement which allows us to choose what we will or will not agree to.

As mentioned before, a belief system is a set of principles that form the basis of what we accept as true to us. One's belief system can be deconstructed just as systematically as it was constructed. Consider this: from the moment that we rise each day, we put on a special pair of glasses, I like to call "perspective glasses." These glasses provide a mental picture of how we believe people should be and operate, based on our own beliefs. For example, my mother does not believe boys should play with toy guns as they may grow up thinking it is okay to shoot people for fun. I, on the other hand, believe that it is fine for them to play with toy guns, and hold that we should train children to inner-stand the proper use of guns. There is no right or wrong answer here, only two perspectives. We choose what resonates with us. In this book, things may come up against your current beliefs. Please inner-stand, it is only your perspective. You get to choose what resonates with you and trash what does not. You may research for yourself or allow others to teach you. Scripture suggests,

"Applaud being open minded while not blindly accepting things"
(Acts 17:11).

For those of you who observe Christmas, remember the good old Santa Clause fairy tale that was basically forced on us since birth? We were told to be good and Santa would reward us by dropping in from a chimney to deliver gifts in our favor. If we really thought about it, most of us probably did not have chimneys. Furthermore, the big, round character that was set to deliver those gifts could not possibly fit through the chimney shoot. Anyway, we readily accepted this fable as truth for a large part of our childhoods and conformed accordingly. We'd change everything about our way of BEing around that time of year. We felt we had to be a certain way so that we could get a certain thing. Most of us became nicer, more sharing and caring, and overall "good girls" and "good boys." Had someone told us that Santa was completely made up, most of us probably would not have been able or willing to receive such truth because it was so embedded in our cultural DNA that he was real. Let's face it, it felt good receiving gifts from this fairy friend! Nevertheless, closing off our minds to new perspectives caused us to give life to the belief of Santa and a host of other false beliefs. The same way the power of agreement worked in the Santa Clause scenario is the exact same way it works in every situation if you care to take an honest look. At first, this was difficult for me to grasp. Especially, when it comes to parenting. I have not always been the best mother, at least in the eyes of others. I subconsciously agreed to the thought of me not being a great Mom which left me sad and defeated. Once I inner-stood the power of agreement, it created a space for me to delete and insert a different narrative, one in which supports my wellBEing instead of depleting my character. Soon after I accepted this notion, I was able to create a story that supported my evolution. Allow me to give you a visual of how I allow the power of agreement to work in my favor.

Around Christmas 2018, I had been homeless for nearly 6 months, living between different places. One of the places was with Aliyah. Going to Aliyah's house was certainly a last option idea because, although she was also my friend, the truth is she was my older sister's best friend. I was hesitant about staying over there considering my sister and I did not get along well, yet there I was relying on her best friend for shelter. During my stay, Aliyah and her Mom cared for me as if I were a long, lost sibling that they had been searching for, for years! Although Aliyah is a phenomenal hairstylist and earns a nice income doing hair, she went as far as sharing in her wealth by providing me the opportunity to do hair and generate income beside her. Aliyah was a very giving sou, in general, and she was a huge influence on my hair business life. With Christmas only days away, I was fortunate enough to have been afforded my first apartment with the support of Adopt-a-Family, which is a nonprofit organization that provides housing and support services for families in West Palm Beach. Before I could qualify for my apartment, I was required to have a job. Being that I already had a security license, working security was the easiest option. On top of that, the place that I was applying for was close to the hotel in which I was living, at the time. I was ultimately employed at Palm Beach State College, a job that I had manifested. We'll get into that shortly.

I did not have a vehicle and was saving to soon get one. I thought it would be wise to get books, clothes and toys from Adopt-a-Family's donations as gifts for Christmas, while using the money I had saved to get a vehicle. Talk about a wise decision. Yeah, right! My children's great-grandmother thought it was the stupidest, weakest excuse for not purchasing the kids toys myself. Oh, and not once, did she let me forget how I was the weakest excuse for a mother. If only you could imagine the amount of pain that her words caused me. I felt like my heart was ripped out of my chest. Speaking with Steve Voyard, a great friend of mine who was my coach in transformation at the time, he asked why I was upset? I had just let him read a message she had written to me. "Steve," I questioned, "did you just read what that lady said to me?" He said yes, and turned it back to me and asked why was I upset? "Is it because on some level you agree with what she is saying?" Yes, that is what it was. I did somehow agree with what she had said about me. I never wanted this for myself, let alone for my children! I had beaten myself up numerous times regarding the poor mother I had become. However, during my time of homelessness, I had to apply what my magnificent mentor Lisa Nichols taught me - to forgive and be gentle with myself, while growing into the mother I intend to be. I changed my narrative. Just because my kids' great-grandmother saw me as a weak excuse for a mom didn't mean that I had to agree. Instead, I chose to redirect my thoughts and support my well-being. I agree that I may not be the perfect mom, if there is such a thing, however I have not given up on becoming the best that I can be! Like the phenomenal Dr. Maya Angelo said,

"Do the best you can, until you know better, when you know better, do better."

I am learning, growing, and doing a lot better because of my evolved belief system. I jumped in the driver seat and changed the direction of my typical path, which used to be the familiar voice of self-doubt. Finally, I took command of my inner voice and told myself empowering things without leaving out the truth. The only voice that truly matters. I gave myself an honest self-evaluation. I wasn't quite where I wanted to be as a mother. In fact, I was nowhere near. I had little to no money, I was forced to let my kids live with my Mom, practically since birth. I know that there is no manual to being a mother and therefore the only way to learn is through experience. I also know that I am not exactly where I want to be therefore, I will continue seeking resources to assist me in my parental development.

Remember, my friend, you have the full authority to decide whether or not you will agree to the information in which you are exposed to, especially as it relates to what people say about you. Your beliefs are yours alone. You chose to adopt them into your being. You have the power of agreement, at play. I encourage you to embrace it and use it wisely.

CALL TO ACTION: Activating Your Power of Agreement

Think of a time you allowed someone's opinion of you to dictate your mood for the day. Do you inner-stand that, on some level, you chose to agree with their beliefs? The great thing about the Power of Agreement is that we get to decide on what we are going to believe. Here's your chance.

1. Change the narrative. Like the Director of your own movie, direct your reality as you see fit.
2. Give yourself an honest self-evaluation.
3. Think about what your updated belief is. Speak that new life into yourself /the situation.

Victim to Witness Concept

Train People How You Want to Be Treated

Have you ever found yourself of the mindset that everyone was against you or purposely trying to hurt you, thinking bad things always happen to you? Have you sought outward approval to justify your worth, or have you been unable to solve problems or even cope effectively with them? Maybe you believe that you, alone, are targeted or mistreated. Do you allow others to take control of your life, or worse, you let your negative self-beliefs sabotage your choices in life? Because of your lack of inner-standing as to the reason a certain event took place in your life, you ask, why me? Perhaps you have been living in regret. These, my dear, are all symptoms of a Victim Mentality. Now, I know that no one wants to be perceived as a victim, yet this is how we unintentionally vote to be perceived. Once we are faced with the truth that we are indeed playing victim, we tend to get defensive and do everything in our power to prove our righteousness. I have come to realize that we all play victim to a certain degree. It is okay to recognize that this is what you've done. The key is to be aware when you fall into victim mode and shift into a witness mentality. Throughout this chapter, take a moment to ponder the times when your beliefs were being triggered. This is when we get to unlock and reveal our ugly truths. Let's face it, we all have something about ourselves that we are not too fond of. It could be a physical, spiritual, or intellectual characteristic. Instead of addressing the issue head-on, we tend to go around it, dress it up, or even put make-up on it in order to mask those ugly areas from what they truly are. Others see the costumed renditions of who we are, during those situations, and not our true selves. Wouldn't you agree that people see the masked version of you, far too often? Check this out. Here is a lifesaver for you, friend. Try it on for size. Instead of covering up areas of your life in which you desire some sort of improvement, stop your drowning and float atop the ocean of victimization, and simply become a witness to the things that are happening around you.

Victims Make Accommodations for Their Victimization

There were times I have found myself practically living in Victim-ville. I felt like everyone was out to get me. My Mom and I were like oil and water. My oldest sister and I did not get along. My boyfriend of 5+ years and the father to my two children treated me as just another girl in his collection. Because of all this drama, in February 2017, I was diagnosed with post-traumatic stress disorder (PTSD). The doctor had given me pills to make me happy, which I thought was the craziest thing

I ever heard! I've always recognized myself to be the happiest, friendliest, and most high-spirited individual I knew. These people have medicine for everything, but I never imagined that I would need meds to make me happy. The trauma that I was experiencing had a lot to do with the way that I was being treated by both my Mom and my children's father, who was untrustworthy and extremely abusive, mentally and physically. My heart was like an open cut needing to be healed. I had brought two beautiful and extremely intelligent children into the world, yet I was broke and broken! How could this be? I never thought I would feel broken. Afterall, I had intentionally gotten pregnant so that I could have someone to show me the unconditional love that I was missing. These children that I birthed to fill my void were here, but the fact remained that their presence did not fix any of the issues that I was dealing with. Quite frankly, it complicated things. Now I had to learn to give unconditional love, meanwhile I was seeking it. When my son was one year old, and my daughter was two. I was living in the family house that my granddad had built from the ground up. With only a two-week notice, I was told that the house was up for sale and that we had to move elsewhere. My Mommy instincts kicked in right away. I knew I had to find shelter for my children and me! I reached out to my friend Trudy to ask if we could move into her apartment in Daytona Beach until I received my income tax check, when I would be able to get my own apartment. It seemed like the perfect opportunity because she had just moved in with her boyfriend and she needed someone to help cover the bills at her vacant apartment. Upon telling my family about the move, they were unsupportingly insensitive and downright nasty. They passionately affirmed that they had absolutely no faith that I can be a good mother without them being close. With their inconsiderate responses, I was more determined than ever to get away from them and prove that I could be a good mom without their assistance. Resolved to make a change in my situation and see an improvement in my relationship with my kid's father, I decided to make the 200-mile move north. I imagined peace would be found in Daytona Beach. My thought was that I would no longer be a burden on my family and that my man and I would work out better, because he would finally be faithful due to the new environment. Interesting concept, I know. Of course, things did not happen as I had hoped. Instead, I found him talking to another woman, which led to more physical fights. After a few months of living in Daytona, I found myself on the bathroom floor crying nearly every day. Each time I looked in the mirror, I saw this unrecognizable woman. I wondered who in the world was this woman staring back at me. I had gone from everyone's favorite to being someone's stepping stool. I was physically, emotionally, and spiritually drained. I had been the sole source of income, working three jobs to sustain our household and provide for my family. I did enjoy my job at the Youth Detention Center for sexual predators, but, working all of those jobs and trying to keep it together was too much. Nevertheless, at the detention center, I had the opportunity to learn about Maslow's Theory, and how trauma and triggers affect the human mind. I was able to establish a good rapport with the teens and hear their truths. Despite my enjoyment with my employment, in the scheme of things, I had run out of excuses as to why I should go on living like this anymore. Something had to give, and it did.

One day, I received a phone call that one of my favorite cousins had overdosed while trying to commit suicide. That was my tipping point. Right then and there, a decision had settled in my soul. I needed to be home. What sense did it make for me to stay in Daytona Beach, mistreated, unappreciated, lonely, and helpless? I was independently supporting my clan and running myself ragged, when I could be home and things could be better. I was tired of being the punching bag for others! When it is all said and done, I did have a family in West Palm Beach that I needed and who needed me, despite our poor relationship. They, at least, stayed ready to support me with my children. And, I was ready to be of support. I had always been the one person that my cousin felt comfortable talking with about her issues. Her making an attempt to end her life made me start wondering if it was because I had not been around that she felt she had no outlet. I was totally distraught. I packed up all that I owned, told my kid's father we were moving back to West Palm Beach and that I was separating from him for good, and we were gone.

Now, I was back at my Mom's house. Instead of my sister and I sharing a room like before, my kids and I now had to share a room with my Mom. Don't get me wrong, I love my Mom. It is just that she and I did not quite have the best mother-daughter relationship so that arrangement was sure to be difficult. Anytime I tried talking to her, we always seemed to bump heads. She maintained the attitude that she was the mother, and I was the child, even though I was a mother myself. Sure, I was young, and yes, her child, but I still had some of my own ideas about what I wanted for my children and for my life. Unfortunately for me, my Mom believed that she was always right about everything, including decisions about my children. I was forced to cage my opinion as if my voice did not matter. When I did something that she didn't like, my very own Mom would call me names like stupid and whore. My entire family called me crazy, ignorant, and blonde (as in 'ditzy'). As a child, it hurt me to hear them call me that until I started to agree and accept their statements as facts. I was always the black sheep of the family, and once I accepted that, I was comfortable in that space. Throughout high school, I often ran away so I could be myself without feeling the need to conform. This time was no different. Although my kids and I lived with my Mom, I did whatever I could to stay away. Leaving my kids with my Mom all day, I only came home when it was time to rest, even if that meant spending my day at the park until nightfall. There were times I would come home early to rest and would smell fresh home-cooked food, as I approached the door. My Mom could throw down in the kitchen! I loved her food. I would walk in with my Kool-Aid smile, excited about what's for "our" dinner. Washing my hands to fix a plate, I would be stopped in my tracks. My Mom would say, "why should I let you eat my food? Do not touch my food." Instead of allowing me to eat, she would rather let the food go to waste, literally. It hurt me to my heart because regardless of our relationship, food was one thing I knew was a basic need. I learned that at the detention center, studying Maslow's Hierarchy. To be denied a basic need by my Mom just did not sit well with me. I felt like a stranger on the street, like a burden that just would not go away. Instead of facing my fears, and speaking up about how I felt, I would stumble out of the house, leaving my kids behind so I could deal with my emotions. You see, my logic was to always look strong and to never let my kids see me cry. They couldn't know that their mom was struggling. Although things seemed to be getting worse, day by day, I figured I would put my free time to good use. I signed up for cosmetology school to create a brighter future for my little family. I was always out and about anyway. I attended school from 8:00 am-3:30 pm, went home for 15 minutes to shower, and get ready for work. I was at work from 4:00 pm until the job was done, which was usually around 2:00 or 3:00 am. One day, going through my normal routine, I noticed my house key missing from my keychain. I called my Mom, only to find out that she had given it to Terriah, one of my sisters, because she had misplaced hers. I was highly upset because I had to be at work in the next 30 minutes and I could not be late. I asked her if I could please come get the house key so that I could shower then head to work, and of course, her response was "no can do!" I was fired.

I Must Secure All that I Need if Ever I Shall Succeed

After losing my job I had fallen into another depression! I knew that I would never be successful while living under my Mom's roof and rules, I thought. There was no way out of my spiraling dilemma unless I moved away. As Maslow's Theory of Human Motivation (Hierarchy of Needs) states, in order to achieve self-actualization, one's basic needs must first be met. I needed to make certain that my basic needs were being met. I could not leave that up to my Mom or anyone else, I finally inner-stood. It had to be me.

> Maslow used the terms *"physiological", "safety", "belonging and love",*
> *"social needs"* or *"esteem",* and *"self-actualization"* to describe the
> pattern through which human motivations generally move. This means
> that in order for motivation to arise at the next stage, each stage must
> be satisfied within the individual themselves. Each of these individual
> levels contains a certain amount of internal sensation that must be met

in order for an individual to complete their hierarchy. The goal in Maslow's theory is to attain the fifth level or stage: self-actualization.

https://en.wikipedia.org/wiki/Maslow%27s_hierarchy_of_needs

A person must have shelter in order to think properly, and as a starting point for all other hierarchical essentials. I needed a place to call home plus I also felt the need for love and belonging. I subconsciously put that responsibility on others, when, in reality, only I possess the power to love me enough to know that I am worthy and that I belong.

My high school best friend, Jeremy, contacted me on social media to check in on how I had been after so many years of us not connecting. Of course, I informed him that my life had become a total wreck! I told him that I was in the process of finding myself again and he knew exactly what I meant. He mentioned that he went through his own personal journey of depression and met a guy, who I'll refer to as Mr. Y, who taught him to retake his life. This Mr. Y person taught Jeremy to speak life into himself and purge himself from things that no longer served him. Mr. Y, apparently, was a prophet of self-love and natural cure. I was told that he had the knowledge to address any dis-ease by way of food. Wow! I thought. It sounded to me that this was exactly what I needed! Jeremy told me that he loves everything about me, but what matters and should continue to matter is how I view myself. That was just the word that I needed to hear, and it became the seed that took root to spark my own personal journey of self-love. Jeremy connected me to Sir Mr. Y. The life I had been praying for was finally about to begin! Mr. Y created a program called the Single Moms Program and was allowing 10 single moms to attend for free.99 (free). I was so grateful to be the first student. I would be living with him and his 3 wives, eating 100% vegan meals, learning about true health, and developing my self-value. Upon completing the one-year journey with Mr. Y, I would leave there with a greater self-awareness, heightened self-worth, a healthier body and mind, and owning a successful business. Oh, to add a cherry on top, my children would have the pleasure of being homeschooled! I did not see how it could get any better. After watching his videos on social media, I was READY to end my trauma and learn all that Mr. Y was going to teach about health and healing. When I informed my family of my plans to explore this life-healing opportunity, they thought I had lost my mind. My mother went as far as telling our pastor, who gave me his perspective on why I should not go. He provided me with some knowledge that Mr. Y means *to know* which of course went against our beliefs because we subscribe to the idea that God is the only all-knowing being. This title generated a degree of caution that I did not have at first. I promised the pastor that I would not go there being gullible and changing my beliefs to someone else's. I felt like God was telling me to go, I reassured him. Giggling, he said, God would not tell you something that he did not tell me. That struck a nerve in me, something terrible. How would he know what my and God's conversations were about? I informed my Grandma (G'ma) of my intended move and she absolutely lost it. A side of my G'ma that I had never seen ferociously rose up before my very eyes. She cut in, immediately, "girl, you must not know who I am, and who I know. If you take those kids, I am taking you to court and I am never speaking to you again." Those words hit me like a bullet to my heart. I didn't see the crime in me taking my own children with me. My G'ma was my first love and I felt so betrayed. How could she, of all people, turn her back on me simply because I decided to relocate my family to Atlanta to find myself? I had thought that she would support my journey of self-improvement. I was very wrong. My Dad did not agree with me moving, either, but he promised me this one thing. He said he would support my move if I left my children, until I had more information about the setup. He suggested that I allow the children to stay with family for about a month, go learn a little about the people that I was going to be living with, then come back for the kids once I was settled, mind, body and spirit. I agreed. That sounded like a reasonable idea! There were a few people that loved me, nonjudgmentally, despite their disagreeing with my decision. They were my uncle Larry, his ex-wife Stephanie, and her daughter Taudra. I am so grateful for them and for my Dad's foresight. I was determined to get to Mr. Y's program and I did whatever it took to make it happen.

My car broke down days prior to my trip. Jeremy paid to get it fixed, then the day before my departure, my car was repossessed. I did not let that stop me. No car - no problem. I went as far as catching my first solo airplane flight, a 2-hour ride, all by myself! As terrified as I was, I believed that the promise of a better life was waiting for me on the other side. Nothing was going to stop me, at this point.

Mr. Y was a self-assured man. You immediately felt his confidence in his speech and posture. He dressed regular, though I thought he'd have on some sacred outfit. He did wear a headdress with an ankh emblazoned on the front, but other than that, he sported stuff that other young black men wore, jeans, sneakers, a designer belt. Upon arriving at the Atlanta Airport, Mr. Y's wives welcomed me with warm hugs and smiles. We listened to some of my favorite jams on the way home. They made me feel comfortable. When we got to the house, Mr. Y was there to greet me. "Stand up and turn around", he said, as the other ladies left for the other living room area. Totally weirded out, I asked why he wanted me to turn around. He told me that he was looking to see how my body will tone after fasting. Mr. Y finished, "you are going to be just right." Then, he asked why I was there. I explained that I was there to gain a good inner-standing on how to be healthy and that I was there to find myself again. He asked if I knew why he had picked me from thousands of women to participate with him. "No," I said, "lay it on me!" He explained that this was a business and family was business. He went on to say that he had to make sure the face of the business had nothing but beautiful faces on the cover. That was super weird to me. I was there for a single mom's program, so a lot of what Mr. Y said didn't match up with what the program was supposed to be about. He told me that he was building a nation, and with that being said, that he needed about 10 wives and lots and lots of children. "We will raise them and teach them the true ways of life," Mr. Y asserted. "That's an amazing dream," I said, then brought him back to our initial conversation. I was there to learn and grow, not to become his fourth, fifth, sixth or any wife. I was grateful that I was selected because I had gotten there on my own merit. Although Jeremy had family ties with the Mr. Y, he had not told them I was interested in becoming a student or anything. In which case, neither did I reveal the relationship between Jeremy and me. I did not want them thinking I was there to get close to Jeremy, for I was there only for my own personal journey to self-love. Things became tricky and interesting, at the same time, and extremely fast. Despite the bitter taste around the notion that Mr. Y wanted to get me into his polygamous circle, there were so many sweet aspects of the arrangement. This was the very first time in my life that I had my own room. My thoughts were free to roam uninhibited by the combative or controlling restraints of others. Upon rising, the wives and I would meditate and workout together. Our routine was very welcoming. Once break-fast came at 12:00 pm, we would build, which meant Mr. Y would teach and we would share our thoughts on the lessons.

He basically taught us that we had been lied to throughout our lives. He told us that God lived on the inside of us, and it was up to us to tap into our Godly power and manifest the lives that we so deeply desired. He instilled in our minds that we were ourselves God's walking on earth and that there was nothing more powerful than us. His favorite saying was *what's more powerful than you?* And we would respond, NOTHING! He also taught us how to heal ourselves from depression and other dis-eases that we might encounter, through our food choices. Mr. Y would talk about the detriments of eating dead foods. Basically, he shared that if we consistently ate dead foods, such as animals, manufactured foods, and seedless fruit, we would be left feeling like the death that we consumed. It made sense and was very revealing for me. It was not new knowledge, though. This was the philosophy of the ancient Egyptian physician, architect, high priest, and young ruler, Imhotep. Imhotep focused on using herbs and natural food to heal people of dis-ease. He originated the concept, "let food be thine medicine, medicine be thine food," over 2,200 years before Hippocrates, the so called 'Father of Modern Medicine', was even born, although Hippocrates is often credited with the idea. As I sat in my room, Mr. Y's voice played like a broken record in my head. The truth had sunken into my spirit. The reason I let my children live with my Mom for a period of time was because I was broken! This experience at Mr. Y's allowed me to finally see my ugly truth. With the peacefulness of my environment, my eyes started to open.

For some time, I had established a strong belief that my kid's Dad and I would be together forever. I never saw myself raising my children without him. I subconsciously made an internal agreement that I would not do it by myself. As much as I loved my babies, I just did not see myself being strong enough to raise them alone. I had to swallow what seemed to be the hardest pill ever: I wanted him and I to work out so badly, but the YOUniverse was not being cooperative, and it was because of me. I began putting him before my children. It was crazy! I came to the realization that the reason my mother and I had not had a positive relationship for all of those years was because, instead of creating a healthy life with and for me, she chose to focus on other relationships. That was her M.O. (mode of operation) with me. Now, I was becoming just like her, without even knowing it. Nooooooo! I had become more focused on my relationship with Tyron instead of with my children. Once I was brave enough to open my eyes and speak such truth into my life, I literally felt the chains of attachment break free like the clearing of a clogged pipe! I moved away from my family to grow and build with Mr. Y. While I was learning a lot of great information, I realized I was hurting myself more than I was growing. As the days went on, Mr. Y's hands became like magnets to my body. In his presence, I became extremely uncomfortable. As a diversion, I decided to tell Mr. Y about Jeremy. I told him how proud I was that he played a major role in Jeremy finding peace within himself again. Mr. Y's response was revealing. He questioned why I didn't want him, "the real thing," instead of the watered-down version in Jeremy. Finally, at that moment, I understood Mr. Y's motive and mindset. It was not so much that Mr. Y wanted to mold me into a great single mom, not entirely, but he wanted me to become another one of his wives.

One evening, I noticed Mr. Y and the wife that I was closest with, getting into what seemed like a fight. It scared the life out of me. After the incident, when we were alone, I asked her if she thought he would prevent me from leaving. She replied, "I'm not sure, love, you have to ask the first wife (who was super close with Mr. Y)." Right then, I knew something was not right. She informed me how she and the other ladies had gone from being students to his wives. I refused to be his next victim. I called my best friend, Kayk, begging her to come get me ASAP! I didn't pack my belongings, nor did I inform anyone about my plan to escape and return to Florida until Kayk and her Mom arrived just outside Mr. Y's home. Once they arrived, I grabbed whatever I could and quickly got out of there.

Settling Back in at "Home."

After moving back to Florida and having to live with Mom again, I really started to notice little things that I despised about my situation. My daughter was wearing the same shoes for weeks straight, although my Mom promised to find her other shoes. On a Friday, after being tired of waiting, I went on a search in my Mom's closet for my children's shoes. Super happy to find them, I texted my Mom to let her know that I had located the shoes and was in the process of straightening her closet to better than how I found it. Her response was shocking, but then again, it should not have been. She replied that I better be out of her house by the time she came home. She couldn't be serious, I thought. When she came home, my Mom let me know how serious she was. As I tried gathering my kid's clothes and shoes, she insisted I left anything that she had bought for my children! I had no money to purchase new clothes and shoes for them, so I continued gathering their belongings. My Mom was not having that, so she ran towards me, pushing and shoving me and doing all that she could to prevent me from getting their belongings. If this sounds unbelievable to you, imagine what I was thinking. I called the police who informed me that because the belongings were in her house, I had no right to remove them. Just like that, my children and I were homeless, simply because I didn't want my kids wearing the same shoes over and over, when in fact, they had other shoes. I decided to let the kids stay with her for the time being. It made more sense to maintain their stability, however fractured it was, while I could find a place for us to live. Every day, I did a self-evaluation, asking myself what I did and did not like about each day. Also, I added, what did I believe I could have done to make my day a lot better? Every night, I found myself wondering where I'd be sleeping. I wanted to stay far away from anyone with children. I couldn't handle the fact that I did not have my little birdies under my wings. It would not help me being around others while they enjoyed their children. I knew that for sure. Once I learned about the witness concept, everything started to make sense.

Becoming a Witness

When we give ourselves permission to step out of the situation and simply glance into the situation, we unlock an opportunity to have a different perspective, allowing us to change our actions. This is called The Victim to Witness concept.

I remember when I was afforded a place in Downtown West Palm Beach on 10th Street, which was once a beautiful and historic setting. Ironically, during my stay, this historic setting turned out to be a most violent and dangerous experience. Although I was grateful to be placed in my first apartment with my children, I became more terrified as the days went on. This was not only the street of my first apartment, but the same location where Deonte, my current boyfriend lived. To add the icing on the cake, it didn't take me long to realize this was also the street my kids Dad, Tyron, sold drugs, gang banged and repped as his territory. One casual rising, me and Deonte were sitting outside, having a normal conversation, when Tyron walked by doing a transaction and observed the connection between us. I thought to myself, "I pray this man does not start his B.S." Before he had the opportunity, I went inside preparing for my son's birthday party at Chuck E Cheese. Tyron attended the birthday party, as we were co-parenting. When the celebration came to an end, Tyron did a good gesture by taking us home. Once I got out of the car to say my goodbye, I could still hear the loud piercing sounds of his voice saying, "Don't be having nobody in this house." Those words reminded me of how controlling and manipulative he was, which triggered the victim in me. Oftentimes, I didn't say much back to him, afraid that he would strike me for having a voice. This time around, however, I somehow built the courage to say, "Boy this is my house, I do as I please." And, as expected, he jumped out of his car, pushed me on the ground, held my face in the dirt and told me, "this is my street, if I catch somebody coming out this house, I'm going to leave him where he stands." I never knew dirt could be so salty. Once I gained my strength back, I gathered my things, took my kids and headed into the house. Tyron then lifted his foot making sure he tripped me while I was walking away, causing me to drop everything in my hands. As I slowly picked up my belongings, my tears splashed off the concrete like thick raindrops. Strangely, I was hoping that he would feel sorry for me and apologize. Upon entering my apartment, my daughter Lyri asked "Mom is Dad gone?" "Yes" I replied. "Show me how hard you can kick," she stated. Me looking confused, I threw my foot in the air, trying to entertain her with a smile on my face, knowing she witnessed everything that just happened. "Next time Daddy hits you, that's what you do," she said with anger. Shockingly, I replied "Okay baby." As we started to settle in, I assisted her with showering. We then heard a knock at the door. "I think that's your Dad," I said, jumping up automatically going into defense mode. "No Mom! don't open the door! Go in the room and wait 'til I get out the shower." After hearing those words from my four-year old daughter, I suddenly broke down in tears. If only I allowed myself to vividly scan the problem instead of being a part of it, I would have been better off. Because I allowed myself to play into his manipulative ways, I now had to face the fact that my daughter was also traumatized at the thought of her Dad coming around.

If you are committed to your growth, which I know you are because you're in this substantial conversation, you must be willing to take off your mask of perfection and address your imperfections. In each moment that you find yourself visiting Victim-ville, know that it is temporary, and a possible lesson that needs your attention. In each moment, you get to choose to view things from a different perspective. Give yourself permission to step outside of what is physically going on around you and shift into the mentality of being a witness.

Instead of dwelling on that traumatic experience, I committed myself to witness what was happening around me. I took accountability, spoke my truths, and continuously moved forward toward the answers, allowing myself to realize better outcomes. Not only for me, but also for my kids. Shifting my mentality from one of a victim to becoming a witness of my screenplay, tremendously changed the trajectory of my journey. It allowed me to step outside of my situation, witness what was going on around me, and give myself honest feedback about my role, like a director of a film. For example, I realized that I was in search of love in all the wrong places. I literally created a child thinking she would fill the void that I so deeply longed for. During this eye-opening revelation of my experience, I realized how I had been putting my energy into my children's father at their expense. As much as I hated fighting him, I initiated it many times. I was the one who started being physically abusive, back in high school, when my feelings got hurt. My controlling spirit dictated that things were to go my way or the highway. I hated that about myself. To be completely honest, I remember him telling me a few times that we should not rush into a relationship and stay friends for a while. I did not inner-stand the hold up. If he liked me and I liked him, I did not quite inner-stand the purpose of taking things slow. We practically lived together in high school. Mom would drop me off to his house a few hours before school because she had to get to work early. I also stayed a few hours after school each day once we were done with our extra-curricular activities. Mom even let me stay over a few nights, so she didn't have to get up so early. Although I had a hard time grasping the things that were being revealed to me, I knew change had to start with me. It was up to me to face my ugly truths so I could evolve into the person that I needed to be, for me and for my children. I noticed some generational patterns that I did not like and I committed to end the cycle with me.

Declare today:

- **I am willing to embrace my ugly truths!**
- **I am in control!**
- **I can transcend into the person I've always known myself to be.**
- **I am committed!!**

> **CALL TO ACTION: Shifting from Victim to Witness**

When you find yourself in Victim-ville, give yourself permission to allow the Victim to Witness paradigm shift to work for you. Follow these steps below.

1. Witness the situation. Step outside of yourself and see the whole situation from an outside perspective.
2. Focus your thoughts and energy on seeking the answer.
3. Take accountability. Inner-stand that you have a role in whatever happens with you.
4. Ground yourself.

I want to take the time to celebrate you, in advance, for taking **BOLD** action and becoming your next best version.

It Takes A Community

Community Equals Energic Connections

Community means: a feeling of fellowship with others, as a result of sharing common attitudes, interests, and goals. Have you ever heard the saying "it takes a village?" I added a little twist to it instead of using the word village, I used the word community. It takes a community. Oftentimes, we get so wrapped up feeling the need to do it all ourselves, like that old saying if you want something done, do it yourself. When you think about it, there are only 24 hours in a day, which means you can only do so much in a day. Think of yourself as a cell phone. For you to continue on your daily mission, you will need a charger and an outlet to put the charger into. The community is our charger. It also serves as our outlets. Times when we allow our limiting beliefs about who we are and what is possible for ourselves to get in the way of our daily mission, we can tap into our community, and gain access to what it is we need in each moment - either a charger or an outlet. Perhaps, you need a therapist, an accountability buddy, a friend, or even an elevating buddy, someone who speaks into our possibilities. That's what I mean by a charger. An outlet is someone who is willing to be listening ear, who will hear your heart, without judgment, and just be there for you. I am grateful for Lisa Nichols' Tribe *Motivating the Masses*. After reading Lisa's book *No Matter What!* and taking one of Lisa's personal development courses, I realized I had lots of self-work to do and I was EXCITED about it! Lisa created a Facebook group page where I could communicate with everyone who took the same course, interact, and celebrate each other's wins. In so many ways, the tribe let me know that I was not alone. They were my power source and outlets when I needed those things and I was theirs. Because of my experience and growth, I was eager and determined to meet this Black single Mom who grew from struggling to making ends meet, to breaking barriers to standing on top of her game. Despite the odds, Lisa rose to the occasion and emerged herself from what seemed like impossibilities into possibilities. She is now living a life of faith, love, abundance, and truth, or as she likes to say, a life that is unrecognizable! It is because of her that I saw possibility for myself. I wanted to meet Lisa so badly. This is how I manifested my desire.

I went in for an interview with a beautiful woman named Dominique. She asked me to wait inside her office for just a second. Sitting anxiously, I overheard her discussing her passion for dance with someone else, and I grew even more excited because that too was my passion. I asked, "Excuse me, was that you I heard talking about dancing?" "Yes girl," she responded, "dancing is my passion, if only you knew." "Oh trust me, I have a pretty good idea," I replied. "Dancing is MY passion too, and it gives me life!" We were like the perfect match. Before even talking about the job, I went into detail about myself and where I was in life. I told her that I had just moved into my first apartment and was looking for an investor (a job) to help support my dreams, my children, myself, my car, my apartment, as well as my growing business endeavors, including hairstyling. I carried Lisa's book around like it was my bible, which I explained to Dominique just how powerful and life-changing her book and appearance on *The Secret* had been for me. After resigning from that job, Dominique and I reconnected at what seemed like perfect timing. Lisa had just announced she would be in San Diego California hosting a live life event called SPEAK AND WRITE TO MAKE MILLIONS 2019 for her last time. There was no way I was missing out on this event. I had no idea how, but I knew I would get there. After discussing the idea with Dominique, she booked our room the Moment we had agreed to go. Approximately, three weeks prior to the trip to California, I was completely discouraged. I reached out to Dominique letting her know that I was sorry for any inconvenience that I would be causing but I could not see how I was going to get the money in time to make our trip. And, if I did somehow come across some money, I would need to use the money to do the responsible thing and pay my bills. Girl, that is not happening! You are going on this trip, even If I must lend you the money, she reassured me. I was extremely grateful for her support, however I took her faith in me and turned it into wood to add to my fire. Dominique reminded me that taking care of my bills AND attending Lisa's event were both possible. With two weeks remaining before the big event, I grew extremely focused and intentional. I stayed in contact with Lisa Nichols' tribe through Facebook who went live, made posts and videos about how they too were eager to attend the event, were stepping out on faith, and living in their own possibilities. That gave me all the fuel I needed to keep the faith that I too would be at the event. I kept the faith until I was able to attend SPEAK AND WRITE TO MAKE MILLIONS 2019 and meet Lisa Nichols, which is detailed in the chapter "visualize to materialize."

CALL TO ACTION: Knowing Your Community

Think of a moment when you notice that the faith in yourself is running low. Who do you go to? And, think about those people who you'd rather run from, in times of despair. Both kinds are part of your environment. Your community, on the other hand, is composed of those people you specifically select to be a part of it.

Take a moment to evaluate the people you spend most of your time with.

1. List the top ten people in your circle.
2. Ask yourself, do they fuel your evolution, or do they drain your engine (deposits or withdrawals)? Put a **D** next to the people that constantly make deposits into your life, and a **W** next to people who mostly take withdrawals.

3. Rate each person on a scale 1-10 (1 meaning they do not trust that you have what it takes to create the life you desire. They believe you are disconnected. 10 meaning they are constantly striving as well as encouraging you to continue striving. You share the same spiritual beliefs. They support you and you have synergy with them). When rating your circle, be sure not to give away any charity high number if they have not earned it.

4. Take note of your 8-10's, those are your wood bringers. They recognize when your fire is running low, they know how and when to rekindle your fire.

Did you know that a shark confined in a fish tank will only grow as large as its environment permits (based on the size of the tank)? Well, think of yourself as a shark and the people you surround yourself with determines your growth.

Everything Happens for a Reason

This may sound a little cliche, *Everything Happens for a Reason*, but I am a firm believer that everything does happen for a reason. Who is to say that I am right or wrong? I still encourage you to try this perspective on. What do you have to lose? When I say everything happens for a reason, it is like giving yourself permission to surrender, because whatever happens, there is a purpose behind it.

To know that there is a higher power who knows my greater good allows me to take a step back from the physical world, and view things on a spiritual level. I know this may be tough to employ in certain situations. Nevertheless, if you care to take an honest look at everything that has happened in your life up to this point, maybe you too can see how everything has turned out or is turning out for your greater good. Again, if you care to take an honest look, only then will you be able to see how everything works out for your greater good. I am telling you the truth.

A lot of troubling things have happened in my life up until this point, which made it extremely hard for me to accept, embrace, and learn to love. Losing my relationship with my best friend Tyron, after approximately 8 years, left me completely empty inside. We had two children together which I had to raise on my own. I became homeless on a few different occasions. My family and I did not get along much. I had completely forgotten who I was. I realized I was always in search for love, without even knowing it. I am beyond grateful for my good friend Jeremy who taught me how to ask myself empowering questions in every situation. Instead of playing into Victim-ville, wondering, why do people keep trying me and taking me out of character? I asked myself, what is this situation supposed to teach me? What am I supposed to learn? What role did I play in having this outcome happen? Many times, in considering these questions, it left me in the question. Being in the question allowed me to come clean about why certain events took place in my life. As the scripture so beautifully puts it:

Keep on asking, and you will receive what you ask for. Keep on seeking, and you will find. Keep on knocking, and the door will be opened to you ***(Matthews 7:7)***.

I encourage you to be okay without knowing the immediate answer, all the time. Sometimes your answers will surface right away, while other answers may take some time. The key will be to be patient, keep speaking your desires, and keep believing. I ask God to allow me the wisdom to be aware of the answer when it is presented to me, and the strength to hold on no matter what the answer is. Again, being that God dwells within us all, our answers are already within us. All we need to do is tap in. To begin this process, take a piece of paper and write down two or three experiences that still cause you a great deal of pain - it leaves you asking, why me? Next to each experience, write your "why". When you don't find your "why" you remain a victim to that particular experience (your past). You'll soon see that there is more power in the present moment. I learned a valuable lesson from my relationship with Tyron. I learned how to love myself. I take it that I had to grow through that long meaningful relationship to inner-stand that love starts with me. My parents nor my partner could give me the love I so deeply desired. My children could not do it for me. After reading Lisa's book in the chapter Developing Your Understanding Muscle, I came to an inner-standing that people are only able to love me at the capacity in which they love themselves. Moreover, it is my responsibility to train people how to love me by the way that I love myself. What had been the case was I allowed the voices on the outside to become louder than the voice on the inside which prompted me to stop loving myself. That was then! My Mom would tell me all the time that she misses the old Lexy, her sweet little baby, as if the updated version of me was not good enough. 'What happened to her?" she would ask. I was 22 years young and although my family called me crazy, it wasn't that I was crazy, rather it was that I was dealing with a lot of very painful things at the time. Yet, I am grateful for the experience because I did not know how to love myself and set healthy boundaries until all of that chaos happened. Until I chose to grow through my situation and witness how I had been responding, I was fully accepting victim-dom and dwelling therein. My friend Dr. Mo always says, "your response is your responsibility." That is a powerful statement that reminds me of the power of choice. It was the growing through that caused me to choose to accept, embrace, and love my hurt. I grew so obsessed with my personal growth that it caused me to want to share my good news with the world! All that I have learned and am currently practicing is now yours to learn and experience. I have come to inner-stand that everything happens for a reason, and so it was. We must accept what is, in order to grow through. Let's go to the drawing board.

Oftentimes, we tend to think things just keep happening to us. And we have absolutely no control over it. We always seem to run out of money, bills are always due, our relationships stink, were constantly sick, nobody supports us, our lives are a living hell, etc. Truth is, we ARE in control and we DO have the power within us to physically transform our current reality at any given time. When you notice yourself dwelling in "why me" mode, allow this action step be the go-to tool in your tool box as you're building that next best version of yourself.

CALL TO ACTION: Finding A Solution

1. Close your eyes and take 3 deep breaths.

2. Draw a line down the middle of the page.

3. On the left side write about an experience from your past where something negative has happened to you, and you felt you had no control. Leaving you in the question "why me?"

4. On the right side of the paper, write out your "why" (With honesty and compassion).

Speak Life into Existence

Now, I want you to really be with me here. Let's talk about the power of our words. If you embrace this one chapter alone, you can shift your reality into one that will better serve you.

Let's go this way…What if each of us were born with a superpower - the power to speak life into existence? Wouldn't that be cool? Guess what? We are! I mean think about it. Have you ever exclaimed that something was going to happen, and BOOM, it happens just as you said it would? Or, have you ever thought or talked someone up? Then, you may say something like, "that's crazy, I was just thinking about you." It was not crazy, at all. That's because we sometimes tap into our superpower without even knowing. It is no coincidence, and in fact, it is perfectly designed that way. The best thing is that we don't have to be pastors, prophets, gurus, or any of such to tap into this power. The Bible says we must speak truth, not deceit and use the power of our tongues to move mountains - our mountains (which can be translated into obstacles, hurdles, problems, situations, and the super famous, circumstances). Scripture puts it this way:

*For "Whoever desires to love life and see good days, let him keep his tongue from evil and his lips from speaking deceit; (**1 Peter 3:10**).*

*Truly I tell you, whoever says to this mountain, Be lifted up and thrown into the sea! and does not doubt at all in his heart but believes that what he says will take place, it will be done for him (**Matt 11:23**).*

Once I laid eyes on this scripture, it was like warm milk going down a new born baby's belly. It resonated on a cellular level. Now that I think about it, I have had a few personal experiences that show God's perfect example of speaking things into existence. Referring back to when I was in high school, I remember one day Tyron had a football game. He was a star player on the team and he wouldn't let me forget it. One day, I said, "what if something happens today and causes you not to play as you normally would?" On that exact day, he had to be rushed to the hospital during the game because he had broken his foot in numerous areas. He was then confined to a wheelchair. I was totally unaware about the power of my voice. That was the last thing I wanted to happen. I truly believe that, because I spoke that something might happen to prevent Tyron from playing football, it did.

Take a moment to place your hand on your throat. Notice the thoughts that come up while your hand is resting there. Do you feel anything ? Now make a statement, actually say the words in your head out loud. Do you feel the vibration coming from your voice? Vibrations are sent out into the YOUniverse as a guide of what you wish to have happen. The YOUniverse doesn't differentiate good or bad, desirables or undesirables, it simply reacts off of your word choice. While I was living with Aliyah, I went to my Moms to visit my children. I noticed they were eating cheese, which ticked me off because I asked both my parents to keep them away from dairy. Dad told me that I'd better take them with me if I wanted to monitor the type of food they ate. I quickly packed a few school uniforms and moved my children with me to Aliyah's. I thank God that she was willing to support me by taking my kids to and from school. I prayed every night and day that the time would soon come when I could be with my kids in peace without disturbing someone else's peace. I wanted to live life the way I always intended: wake up to the sunrise, meditate, workout, engage in daily activities with my children, read to them and brush their teeth before bed. These things were my recurring prayer. After three days had passed, my prayers were answered. Adopt-A-Family, a family-services program in which I had applied for assistance months earlier, had called to say they had identified temporary housing for my family at a local hotel. I chose the option to reside in Lake Worth because I was born and raised there and was extremely familiar with the community. That was, is, and will always be my hometown. Like most people probably would have done, I chose to stay in my comfort zone, which turned out not to be so comfortable. The Travelodge Hotel on Dixie Highway and 6th Avenue had a lot going on, there, to include prostitution, drug deals, and a whole lot of traffic. Both of my parents' families are well known in Lake Worth. So much so that I remember walking down Dixie Hwy on the way to the store to grab a few groceries and a driver stopped in the middle of the road and yelled out the car window, "Ain't you some kin to the Odums?" I said yeah, and he asked what I was doing walking. Then he said the nicest thing, "Don't you know you are royalty? This is your city! Someone should be carrying you around." With all that had gone on with my Mom, that man's word made me feel special. I knew how known both the Meeks and Odums clans were in Lake Worth. My great-granddad, P.W. Odums, was the first black police officer in Lake Worth FL. He was also a builder. Granddad had built several buildings in the city. The Odums family was known for being great givers, awesome builders, savvy businesspeople, and overall well-spirited people. Our families were huge. My Great granddad P.W. had 9 children and my granddad, Herbert Meeks had 9 children, too. They alone pretty much took up the small city of Lake Worth. The Meeks side of my family were known for getting in trouble, getting in trouble, and getting in more trouble. LOL! But, seriously, *trouble* was their middle name. They were also known for being extremely talented at almost any sport, and this side of my family was also great at business. My thinking was that was their lifestyle. I had to find my own way and become financially stable the best way that I knew how. I was grateful for my gift of doing hair. It has been a blessing, providing me with a way to earn the funds to handle the things that I had to handle. I can't lie, although I felt like a piece of trash, for the most part, walking down Dixie Hwy that day, those words were reassuring ! He was right about one thing; my family is like royalty in Lake Worth. Unfortunately, I am the black sheep. As I raced back to the hotel from the store, I noticed a homeless man following me. Scared out of my mind, I started to speed up. "Excuse me," he said. I looked back and said, "I'm Okay." He continued "Excuse me?" I stopped in my tracks, remembering the stories my Mom used to tell me about a younger me running up to homeless people and hugging them and spreading love. It is sad that over time, I had grown so far from that precious, forgiving, and loving child. "Yes?" I responded. Pointing at the hotel, he asked if that was where I was living. Had he been watching me? Looking stunned and puzzled, I answered, "Yes, I do, why do you ask?" Have you seen *The Secret*, he asked? "What secret?" I responded. "It's a movie on Netflix, it would be perfect for you, it will be the key to get you out of your situation." Looking confused and thinking to myself, if he knew the key to get out of a bad situation, why hasn't he himself taken the advice and built a good life for himself? I just responded, No, I didn't, I don't watch T.V. dear." He did not give in. "Okay, once you get the opportunity, be sure to watch it. It would be perfect for you to watch, but it scares the life out of me." Looking even more confused, it was like he had read my mind. I don't get it. How on earth is he offering a movie that will somehow help me out of my situation when he's too afraid of allowing it to help himself? As I went back into the hotel, something kept telling me the guy coming to me with that movie was no coincidence. I went ahead and signed up for a Netflix 7-day free trial, searched for *The Secret*, and I watched intently to see why this homeless man recommended it. I tell you, my life has never been the same, since. Have you ever heard the saying once you know, you can't unknow? The awareness I received resonated on every level. *The Secret* is essentially describing the Law of Attraction. The movie spoke about how one's thoughts become their reality. What you think and thank about, you bring about. Your life is a physical manifestation of the thoughts that go on in your head, Lisa Nichols stated. The more you show appreciation for the things you already have, you draw in more things in which to be grateful. The movie had multiple individuals share their stories about how they used the law of attraction to work in their favor. A woman spoke about how she cured herself from breast cancer by focusing her thoughts on that which was positive. She visualized herself being healed completely, until that became her reality. Whatever we think about and speak about, we bring about. After seeing Lisa Nichols, a Black Queen, speaking about this stuff, I just knew it had to be true. For the very first time I felt a wave of knowing and inner-standing seep down into my soul. That was my aha moment! We create our lives by the things we think, say, and do. I ask you again, from earlier, can you think of a time that you have said something, and it happened just as you said it would. I began to have flashbacks of how I subconsciously speak life into existence regularly. Most times, it is unconscious, too. I think about how I always say that I am always rushing. And, sure enough, I find myself rushing each and every time. Have you ever heard parents say to their children that they are going to be just like their dad or mom, whichever the 'bad' parent is? Over and over, that child hears that until he or she embodies the qualities of the vilified parent and turns out "just like them." We predestine things with our words. Have you heard yourself saying any of the following or similar statements that have ended up being self-fulfilling prophecies? I can't get that job or my own place. My credit score is always crap. I stay broke and cannot afford to buy anything nice. I am going to be late to work and lose my job. Nothing is working for me. Or, how about this one? I am not worthy of love.

Watch your words, for they can write life or spell disaster. We must be careful what we say. More specifically, we must be mindful of how we are spelling the words of our life's narratives. The Bible says:

*Death and life are in the power of the tongue: and they that love it shall eat the fruit thereof (**Proverbs 18:21**).*

To my inner-standing, that means our words can be like casting a spell. Therefore, we must monitor what we say, because regardless of if the words are positive or negative, they shall come forth. If we believe with all our heart whatever is coming out of our mouths, and direct our words more meaningfully, we get to create our world as we desire it.

From elementary through my 7th grade year, I was in honors classes. Very smart girl, I'd say. However, my family thought it would be okay to upgrade from calling me stupid to blonde and I wore it like it was a badge of honor. Until one day, my aunt asked me to go get a pack of plates for our family function. I joked, "auntie, you know I'm blonde and you can't send me to the store because I might come back with something totally different." She said, no you're not, girl you are smart as ever. Stop speaking that over your life!" It is as if a light bulb had gone off in my head at that very second. She was right! I am smart! I had bought into that lie for years and now I knew better. What words have you been feeding yourself that you are ready to shake free from?

CALL TO ACTION: Speaking Life into Existence

(Mirror Work)

1. Close your eyes. Take 3 slow deep breaths.
2. Think about something someone has said to you, or you have said to yourself that no longer serves you.
3. Bring to mind your replacement belief of yourself.
4. Once you have it, open your eyes, and say your replacement belief out loud.

For example: I am smart, in fact I am BRILLIANT! You may use this:

I am brilliant. I am powerful. I have what I say. Everything that I desire shows up in my life. I only manifest positive and miraculous results. I have unlimited possibilities at my command. I am physically, mentally, and spiritually strong.

If you need some help figuring out the truth about you, here are a few things God says about you:

> *But you are a chosen people, a royal priesthood, a holy nation, God's special possession, that you may declare the praises of him who called you out of darkness into his wonderful light* (**1 Pet 2:9**).

> *I praise you because I am fearfully and wonderfully made; your works are wonderful, I know that full well* (**Psa 139:14**).

Or you can connect with someone in your community whose opinion you trust. You know that this person will tell you nothing but the truth, and they will remind you of all the greatness that lies within you.

Don't be afraid to scream it to the top of your lungs! Say it over and over until your spirit believes it. Sometimes we have to speak things over and over to trick our minds into believing what our spirits are crying for rather than what is actually happening in our physical world. It took repeated speaking and repeated hearing for you to accept the lies. So, what you hear and say can and will become truth. FACTS: The words we speak produce life and death.

So then faith comes by hearing, and hearing by the word of God.
(Rom 10:17).

I remember just before my 90-day mark of living in the hotel, the company required me to have a job with steady income prior to them helping me move into my own apartment. I created a vision board of all the things I wanted to see come into fruition. On that vision board, I had a picture of a security guard at Palm Beach State College and a picture of the beautiful Lisa Nichols, who I was now crazy about after seeing her on *The Secret* and reading her best seller, *No Matter What!* I also had a picture of a beautiful yoga teacher and the car that I wanted, on my board. Two of those visions have come to life thus far. I had been meditating on what it would be like working at Palm Beach State College, visualizing myself driving the golf carts saying "10-4" or "copy that" over the radio. Although I did not know the duty of becoming part of the security team, I did know that security officers communicated through radio using the phrase "copy that." After about a week or two of meditating on this job, I received a phone call from Palm Beach State College with an offer for employment. Upon completing the interview process, I was ordered to take a drug test. I did not pass. Another week or two went by and I received another call from the college asking if I still wanted to be hired as a security officer. I said, "wait, I thought you guys said I didn't pass the drug test." He said, it says here that you have passed. Totally weirded out, I accepted the offer!! This was the law of attraction at play. I had put so much energy into seeing myself as a security officer at Palm Beach State College that it superseded reality. I believed it so much so that it had to happen, and it did. Now, I know this may sound a little woo woo to you. That is because it is new-new, and that is okay. I am extending you the invitation to just try it for yourself.

In 2017, my heart was completely crushed and destroyed when my doctor notified me that I was diagnosed with HSV-2. I was in total shock and felt disrespected that he would even say something like that about me. "This has to be a mistake, sir. Can we do a blood test to be sure that, that's what it is?" I asked. He reassured "Ma'am, I'm 100% positive that that is what it is." It sounded like he was speaking gibberish! How in the hell did I get herpes, I thought? I have only been with two people other than my kid's father, and, to my knowledge both were "clean." How could this be? Feeling betrayed, angry, and hurt, I was completely shocked out of my mind! This is Lexy, we're talking about - the smart, sexy, popular, school athlete that the world was in love with. She couldn't have herpes! The idea didn't even sound right! Questions began to flood my mind. Out of everybody in the world, how in the hell do I have herpes? I know the doctor says it's very common that almost 1 in every 4 people contract herpes, but ME? It couldn't be me! How am I going to tell my partner? My family? The world? This was NEVER supposed to be.

It was never supposed to come down to this. Wow! This was around the time I met Mr. Y and his several wives. I shared a beautiful connection with one of Mr. Y's wives, Sasha, who was a direct reflection of me and also Capricorn. Being in the kitchen assisting her with cooking alkaline dishes as well as following Dr. Sebi's teachings and guidance, I was equipped with the knowledge that I needed to (1) know that I was not alone, and (2) heal myself naturally. Instead of claiming that I have herpes, I begin to say I am healed. With that confession of healing, days turned to weeks. Weeks turned to months. Months turned to years. I continued to pray that God would reveal to me the meaning behind this whole plot twist. One day a familiar voice whispered, "it is not about you baby, it is so much bigger than you. You had to grow through this to be a light to show others how to be resilient, how to be mindful of your sex partners history, and best of all to be an example that all things are curable from within." Instead of asking why me, I started asking why not me. I learned to surrender and allow the all-knowing spirit to use me. Over and over, I heard it loud and clear. "IT HAD TO HAPPEN TO ME, LEXI!" I am someone who can get the message across, bravely and unashamedly enough to let others know they are not alone! I am someone who chooses to be strong enough to live out loud. That is me. You too can evaluate the areas of your life which are challenging and adopt the perspective that everything happens for a reason. Ask yourself powerful questions, pray for wisdom, and ask for the awareness to know the answers once they appear. Pray. Meditate. As long as you are open to receive, your answers will be shown to you. As it so beautifully states,

> *Ask and it will be given to you; seek and you will find; knock and the door will be opened to you* ***(Matthew 7:7).***

With years of continuous application of this perspective, it finally came to me in the smoothest way ever. I was deeply in love with Deonte at the time, yet my spirit kept telling me to be with my ex-boyfriend, Wallace, someone I had been with since before Tyron. This calling had to be the weirdest thing I have ever heard my spirit tell me because I knew, without a doubt, that I did not see Wallace in the same way anymore. For whatever reason, my soul was screaming his name. It kept telling me that I can be with him and the feelings would come with time. I did just that. Breaking Deonte's heart, I went with my divine instruction. As we laid in bed watching a movie, I noticed Wallace trying to initiate sex with me. I stopped him in his tracks, telling him that he knew my situation and I did not want to have sex until I was healed! He snapped back, "What!? That doesn't make sense when I have it too." It felt like a ball of fire had dropped from my heart to my stomach. He had never mentioned this before. "You what?" I quickly sat up in bed. He said, "you think you're the only one who has it?" "Yoooooo!" I screamed. "This is all making perfect sense now! It was you! You're the one who gave this to me years ago." Wallace was in denial, of course. I let him know that I was in search of the answer since I was diagnosed as to who in the hell gave this to me in the first place. My answer has just been revealed. Wallace finally agreed and apologized for being careless. I have said all that to say plant yourself in the question of things, follow your intuitive nudges, and the right answers will be revealed to you.

88

Eye Create Abundance

Have you been drowning yourself in coulda - woulda - shoulda? Do you find yourself hoping, wishing, and dreaming, or even praying, yet you haven't been seeing any results? What if I told you that you could be, do, or have anything your heart desired? I am not talking about only in one area of your life but in every area of your YOUniverse. Truth is, we get to have it all! As children, the people before us tell us, "You can do anything you put your mind to." Now that I think of it, they were absolutely right! Whatever goes on in our physical world first holds space in our mental world. Think about a time you wanted to be, do, or have something that seemed challenging to obtain. You had no idea where the money would come from, or how you would have achieved the very thing that you were seeking. Somehow, you were able to physically gain possession of it. That is because energy grows where energy goes. Meaning, whatever you give focus to gets all the attention.

Energy Flows Where Energy Goes

Have you ever thought about someone, or something and then, BOOM! you receive a letter, a phone call, or even a visit from that person sooner than later. It happens every single time whether you're intentionally trying to attract something positive or seeking to avoid negative things. Whatever you hold onto with your thoughts and feelings, that is what will manifest. Therefore, we must be careful to hold onto thoughts about the very things we truly desire and let go of anything that does not align to that. When we do not master over our thoughts, the ideas that are allowed to seep in will determine our circumstances. James Allen said it best, "circumstances do not make a man, they reveal him." What that means is you are NOT your circumstances, but your circumstances are a reflection of your thoughts. Allen says, "A man cannot directly choose his circumstances, but he can choose his thoughts, and so indirectly, yet surely, shape his circumstances." When circumstances show up, they reveal our recurring thoughts or beliefs. For example: I found myself in many broken relationships that resulted in me feeling a sense of loss in direction. I did not know what to do next. It was challenging to release because of attachment. I could hardly recognize the woman I had become. So, to take responsibility of my circumstances, I began asking myself powerful questions. What is this challenge teaching me? What am I doing to have this challenge show-up? What do I see missing from this challenge that I get to add, such as compassion, inner-standing, the need to act, or simply love? Love always wins. Now that I know what I do not want, I can begin to manifest the things that I do want. First, we must get clear about what it is that we want to create in our reality. Then we must align our thoughts to what it is we desire. If you say you want peace and happiness to overflow in your life, then you must focus your thoughts on the things that bring you peace and happiness. Let go of anything that does not align with your peace and happiness, my friend. Your results are a physical manifestation of the thoughts that go on in your head, as Lisa Nichols states. Now, this isn't some woo-woo, witchcraft, shaky danky type theory. This is a universal law, called the law of attraction. Just like there is a law of gravity, though it is invincible, it is still very present. This is no different. Now, hopefully you have developed an inner-standing that things don't just happen to us, in fact, our thoughts transmute themselves into our reality/physical world. We need to get clear about what it is we want to have happen in every aspect of our YOUniverse. Here's how I utilize this perspective. When I heard that Lisa Nichols would be hosting an event called in 2019, I was determined to be there. I had absolutely no idea how I would get enough money to cover a $300 flight, approximate $400 hotel expense, $300 admission fee, and still cover all my regular household expenses. Nevertheless, I knew one thing for sure; I would be in that building, taking pictures with Lisa, learning how to become a best-selling author and phenomenal speaker, and developing myself overall. I held on to that thought, relentlessly. Replaying in my head what it would be like meeting the woman who helped me help myself for the very first time! I created a vision board like the one I had seen in *The Secret*, putting Lisa's picture in dead center, I placed a San Diego sticker directly under her picture next to the words SPEAK AND WRITE TO MAKE MILLIONS APRIL 25, 2019. I also placed a dollar bill which I added three zeros to make it a thousand-dollar bill, which was the amount needed for me to have a successful trip. I received a call from Diamond, a woman working in the HR department at Platinum Security, "I haven't forgotten about you dear I've been pretty busy lately, now that I'm no longer working a night job, I have a little room to breathe and would love to meet up with you". It was as if God directed her in my life at the perfect time! Anxious to finally meet with her to discuss our goals about me becoming an entrepreneur, I thought it would be a perfect time to also invite her to Lisa Nichols event. That's exactly what I did. The feedback I received from her was everything I could imagine. She's a risk-taker, who loves to travel and learn. The perfect duo I thought. It was like we were soul sisters. Two weeks leading up to the event I had come up with $500 by doing hair , I realized my dream was actually becoming a reality, I took another leap of faith and paid $150 which was half the amount for the entry ticket. Using my payment as a grounding tool to manifest enough funds to complete my purchase. I put the remaining of the money towards the bills at home, securing shelter for my children and I. As the days flew by I grew discouraged and was all out of solutions. It seemed as though one thing went wrong after the next. At this point I had given up on trying to attend the event. Instead I put all my energy into making sure my children and I always kept a roof over our head and did not become homeless again. Now I know I'm no expert in money management in fact nowhere near. However, taking this trip in the midst of moving didn't sound like the best move. Once I decided I would not be attending the event, I reached out to Diamond who insisted we meet up at a local McDonalds. Once she arrived, I shared my concern with her and informed her about my decision to not attend the event. She inhaled deeply. "What! Girl you ARE going on this trip even if I must pay for it and you pay me back later. You have to go. You are the one who introduced me in the first place, and I know how much you love this woman." My heart quickly filled with joy at the possibility of seeing the woman who helped me change my mindset from one of lack to one of abundance. This scene reminded me of a chapter in Lisa's book that spoke about borrowing someone else's faith until you're able to see that same possibility within yourself. That's exactly what I did. I reconnected with the possibility that I get to do BOTH ! All I had to do was release my old stinking thinking and replace it with thoughts that spoke into my intended outcome. Instead of thinking I can't do both , I thought I get to do both, because that is what I desired and was determined to realize. As the days went by, I continued to speak life into my situation:

Eye create abundance, abundance is all around me, money flows to and through me effortlessly. I am worthy to have all that my heart desires now!!

Here we are three days after meeting with Diamond I had earned exactly $1,000! I remember texting my Uncle Larry, informing him about my massive success story! I was in shock at the fact that I was able to receive the exact amount I intentionally placed on my vision board. It was the exact amount needed to secure both challenges, but even more shocking was at how rapidly it all occurred. It was as if abundance had been waiting for me all along, and I was allowing myself to finally receive it. At that moment, I was able to feel my cheeks hurting from smiling. My emotions and senses were stimulated. I envisioned tears running down my face, the welcoming and reassuring embrace of Lisa hugging and squeezing me, me giving her thanks for being a rock and a ray of light who decided to share her story with me. It was because of her bold and courageous ACTION that I was able to connect with my story and stand on it, and not in it. After completing all purchases for the trip to San Diego, I received an email from Lisa inviting me to join her for her son's wedding reception. Now, it was one thing to meet the magnificent Lisa Nichols, but to also be able to meet her baby boy, the very little guy that gave her permission to give herself to the world. That alone would be worth my entire trip!! This worked out beautifully because Diamond and I had already planned to arrive a day in advance. Once we arrived in California, it was like inhaling fresh oxygen. I was surrounded by inspirational pictures, posters, and sculptures, all directing me towards one thing, gratitude. You could not tell me I wasn't in heaven. Everything

seemed so perfect. After arriving at the hotel in an Uber, Diamond and I quickly prepared for the wedding reception. Entering the hotel and requesting to be led to the SPEAK AND WRITE TO MAKE MILLIONS affair felt so natural AND so unreal! I had visualized the feeling I would have once I arrived and man, I gotta tell ya, it was everything I could imagine and more. Taking it all in, while following the signs toward our event, I heard someone say Hi Ms. Meeks! I looked over and saw a sweet lady named Vivian that I had met in Lisa's support group on Facebook. Moving closer to the entrance, lots of others also began to recognize me. Many came over to love up on me. It felt like a warm welcome home. While

crying at the idea that I was there to be a part of the event Lisa Nichols was hosting, a beautiful soul by the name Kim came to comfort me and let me know that I was not alone, and that she gets it! Once Lisa arrived, Kim asked me if I wanted to get a picture with Lisa. Before I can get the full YES out, I was cheek to cheek with Lisa Nichols, taking that picture.

This reminds me when, after living in a hotel for 3 months, I envisioned my children and I living in a 1 or 2 bedroom apartment. Then, I received the news of being blessed with a 3bedroom. I couldn't see how my life could turn out any better. I remember telling Morris, now, all I have to do is get a 4-bedroom so that I can have an office, and then another bedroom for when DeMari gets big enough to have his own room. A week before moving into my home, I received a phone call. The woman who was supposed to take a 4-bedroom place no longer wanted it and it was being given to me. It was immediately available for me to move in, should I wish to do so. I gave the resident manager a cheerful, YesYES! There I was, walking into not only my vision but my children's vision also. They always spoke about wanting stairs in our home and BOOM! we got that too. A town house, no doubt. We were thrilled. Isn't it amazing how once I decided to actually see possibility, I was met with abundance! You have the same superpower within you. All you have to do is tap into it and take action.

SPEAK & WRITE TO MAKE MILLIONS *Encore Celebration*

NOVEMBER 1-3, 2019
Newport Beach, CA
WITH
Lisa Nichols

CALL TO ACTION: Manifesting Your Desires

Affirmation: I live a life that aligns to my desires!

1. Using as much detail as possible, write "I desire to...(indicate your desired results)."

2. Visualize yourself already acquiring what it is you desire. Trust and live as if it is already done. Write, "I am grateful now that...(your desired result) has happened."

3. What actions are you now committed to that will create the results you desire? Begin by writing, "I am now committed to…(the actions) until I materialize… (your desired result).

4. After you have completed the above steps, post this sheet prominently where you will see it daily (i.e. on the bathroom mirror), and read what you wrote, with feeling.

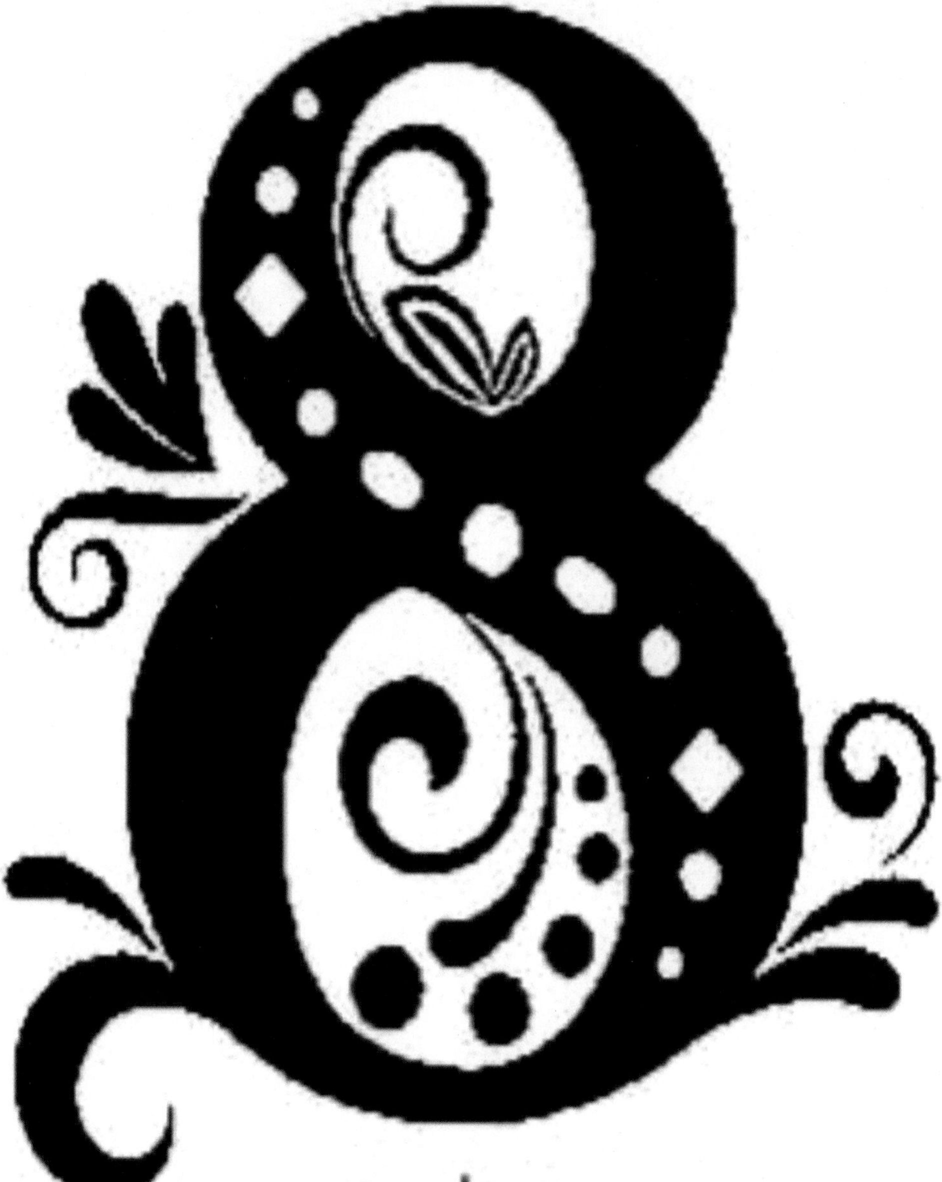

Conscious Choices

Being Aware of Your Decisions

You have the power to create a world where you feel empowered and full of excitement - a world where your heart and bank account is full. You can be surrounded by people who support you, teach you, and act as role models for you while you push yourself to grow. You can have positive relationships with your family grounded in love and mutual respect. You can relocate yourself from operating in scarcity of not having enough, knowing enough, or being enough, to a place of abundance and prosperity by maximizing the areas in your YOUniverse. It can all be done with continuous application of making conscious choices.

Think about it. You make numerous choices in your business and in your daily life. It is important to pay close attention to the choices you make because the choices you make indicate what you value. During challenging times or in a storm, it may seem difficult to pause, reflect, and make conscious choices based on your values. Thankfully, integrity governs the unseen and decisively difficult areas of our lives. Plus, we have the benefit of being able to learn new habits and appropriate responses. Remember, repetition is the mother, father, sister, brother, auntie ,uncle and cousin of learning, and habit creation. How else could we gain the strength to make conscious choices based on our values, except by continuously building on that muscle practicing making conscious choices. Have you heard the saying, "once you know, you cannot unknow?" The moment a challenge arises, you are left with two choices, you can either pretend there isn't a problem, or you can see the problem for what it is and take action. Choices are like keys that unlock doors of opportunity or lock them away. Choices determine how we receive information. Please inner-stand that your entire world is based on your perspective, how you choose to receive and perceive the world around us. It is all basically made up. Our perspectives are based on our personal B.S. (belief systems) and experiences. Don't you ever wonder why different people in the same family practice different religions, subscribe to different ideologies, or maintain different diets. While society dictates what is "normal" or "acceptable" about everything that humans experience, there really are no right or wrong answers. Again, it is all made up. It's always about what resonates and feels good to each person as an individual. While in a neutral state, we must pay attention to how we are going to choose to respond to life's offerings.

Let's take a look at this. Think about all the choices a business owner makes when starting a business. They choose the type of business they want, the vision, values, customers to serve, the products and services to offer, all the way down to creating the prices. Your life works that same way. The more choices you make with consciousness/awareness the more active control you have over your destiny. Are you hoping to one day be successful, or do you actively choose to be successful? Are you conscious about how you respond to challenges and other daily activities? Or, are you running on autopilot? In each moment you get to choose to pause, reflect, notice your body sensations, identify the source of your reaction, and consciously decide to make a choice. The truth is that abundance is always knocking on our doorstep. All we must do is tap into it. We have the power to make conscious choices. Although there are many options we get to choose from, I have narrowed them down to just a few. We have access to choose from what we value (our highest good) or we can choose from a place of comfort, being right, or feeling the need for approval. Choosing the things that support your highest good will give access to people, places, and things that will assist and guide you on your journey and make peace, happiness, and abundance available. We tend to close off doors to opportunity when we make choices that defend and protect our comfort, our need to be right, and our need for approval. We live in could've, would've, should've, and why me mode, always dreaming, hoping, wishing, and waiting on change, when the truth is, we are the change. Our brains are wired to protect us from harm or danger. Recent work by researchers at Stony Brook University revealed that after repeated or prolonged periods of danger, the brain remembers and recognizes threats and dangerous situations. When we are exposed to dangerous situations and feel fear all the time, our brains are trained to keep us on alert. Our brains build walls of protection which causes us to play it safe because our brains are always in survival mode. So it is with being comfortable. We feel the need to do whatever it takes to stay in our comfort zone, defend our righteousness, and secure other's approval. This phenomenon is called fight or flight. The thing is, unfortunately, this natural defense mechanism discourages swaying from the norm and directs all within us to fight or flee change. Put another way, our brains seek to avoid change because there is a risk of the host becoming uncomfortable. The promising thing is this, we were given power and not created with fear, so we can shake it, if we desire.

> *For God has not given us the spirit of fear, but of power and love and of a sound mind (**2 Tim 1:7**).*

We must get clear about where we intend to be in life. Only then can we make conscious choices that defeat fear and support the next best versions of ourselves. To get to that next best version, you must take responsibility for the choices you make.

CALL TO ACTION: Getting Clear on What You Want

Like a GPS, we must begin with the end in mind.

1. Think about how you want your life to be. What do you wish to do, and what would you like to have? During this exercise, do not limit yourself to thinking you must sacrifice in one area in your YOUniverse to gain elevation in the other area of your YOUniverse.
2. Think BIG! We serve a BIG God who wants nothing less than for you to operate in Abundance. Now, the choice is yours. What will you create?

Be in Your Power

Ever noticed that no matter what situation you find yourself in, the common denominator is always YOU? Everywhere you go, there you are. At what point do we say, hmm, "if I did not act, think, or see things a certain way, would I be here?" Are you ready for this chapter?

Stand In Your Authenticity

Have you wondered why after 13 years of schooling, most people cannot seem to recall half the things they've learned? Somehow, however, we can describe when, where, and how, and from whom we received our very first kiss. I believe it is because we remember experiences that involve the whole of us, our minds, bodies, and spirits. I mean, after all, this is who we are. Right? And with a kiss, it is emotional, physical, and spiritual.

I am going to take you back with me down memory lane. I had just become a new mommy to a beautiful baby girl named A'Lyria Sanai back in 2014. Although there was no manual for being the perfect mother, I had a favorite cousin that swore

107

she possessed the blueprint. One of her theories that I did not particularly agree with was, I couldn't be a dancer and a mom, and if so, there's a time and place for it.

Those words pierced me like a knife to my chest! Dancing was my main outlet and I loved doing it. Mind you, 2014 was the year I was chosen for not only a leadership role during my first year as a band member, but I also won an award for Best Dancer. That was huge! Although I had danced with the Dream Team and FBI Kids, the hottest dance group at the time, I had only recently embraced the fact that I was a dancer. Now, to think that I had to let dancing go simply because I had become a mother saddened me immensely. You see, this was my favorite cousin, one that I looked up to in numerous ways. She and I were like twin sisters. I took her advice as if it were fact, and before I realized it, I had stopped dancing for three whole years!

As a result of this conversation between my cousin and I, my life changed as I had subconsciously agreed with her opinion that dancing and motherhood did not go together. I had accepted her perspective and presumably adopted her belief. I convinced myself that my cousin was right. It was time for me to be a role model and apparently, role models were not dancers. After three torturous years for me of not dancing, I found myself in a low and dark place. I missed dancing, incredibly! I notice when I conform to other people's expectations of what I should be doing, I am not happy. At least, I was not when it came to me not dancing. I was not living in my authenticity. This experience showed me that we must be in our authenticity if we are to be free, if we are to be ourselves, and if we are to be at peace.

EYE CREATE ABUNDANCE
Helping people help themselves

CALL TO ACTION: Being in Your Power

1. Write about a time you felt stuck, whether it was at a job, relationship, financial situation etc.

2. Identify the meaning of abundance (in your own words).

3. Visualize the abundance you intend to create in your YOUniverse.

4. Write a sentence or two that describes the abundance you intend to have in each part of your YOUniverse (your career, finances, health, relationships, community, etc.).

5. Dwell (meditate) on the images that come up in your mind from your sentences.

6. Now, enjoy the feelings that you are experiencing.

About the Author

*E*lexis *M*eeks, also known as *A*jai *A*lai, which means *Be In Your Power* is a passionate transformational speaker who stands on the philosophy, "Eye Create Abundance." During her personal life's journey, Elexis has gathered tools to assist in building and creating the life that she loves. Ms. Meeks is committed to being the butterfly ripple effect by being Authentic, Transparent, and Loving, and making her desires non-negotiable. She maintains the expectations of continuing to blow her own mind and help others in the process.

Mentored by the likes of Lisa Nichols and Lakiesha Michelle, and having been trained through GRATITUDE TRAINING, MASTERFUL LIVING, AND SPEAK AND WRITE TO MAKE MILLIONS, Elexis has a wealth of knowledge, skills, experience, and resourcefulness.

Ms. Meeks is the CEO and Founder of Eye Create Abundance, where she is the container for a powerful transformation into your next best version. Elexis is a mother of three, transformational trainer and coach, entrepreneur, and dancer. With this book, INTO ME I SEE, her first offering, Ms. Meeks adds to her credits, published and soon-to-be, Best-Selling author.

www.EyeCreateAbundance.com   @EyeCreateAbundance

Made in the USA
Columbia, SC
28 October 2020